quiet
your
inner
critic

A Positive Self-Talk Journal

BY LINDSAY KRAMER

CHRONICLE BOOKS
SAN FRANCISCO

Introduction

Take a moment to reflect on why you're here. On how you arrived at this page on this day in this moment. Maybe journaling was recommended to you by a friend, loved one, or professional. Perhaps this was a gift, and you're just curious to see what it's all about. Or, it could be that you're here because you're determined to learn how to do what the journal suggests: quiet your inner critic. Regardless of what led you here, the exciting part is the possibility waiting in these pages—possibility that can lead to great changes in your life.

In my work as a psychotherapist, I ultimately serve as a supportive figure to guide others through a variety of life stressors. Everyone has unique stories and wounds, but many clients share inherent common-alities: They are hoping to disconnect from some form of negativity and, in turn, embrace a greater sense of joy in their lives. If you're like most people in our culture, you have to deal with the ultimate conundrum of how to "live your best life" and be your happiest self, 24/7. Many of us strive to have it all and operate at our fullest potential. We have meetings, playdates, bucket lists. We use online platforms to express our opinions. We struggle to slow down and savor the present. We don't take time to appreciate ourselves.

In the process of navigating our lives, we're constantly experiencing an internal commentary about our past, present, and future. Many call this act "self-talk." This journal will serve as a tool to help transform your own self-talk and its influence over your life.

There's something truly powerful about self-talk. When we repeat something enough, its message becomes programmed in our minds. For the most part, self-talk manifests itself into two types: negative self-talk and positive self-talk. If you've sought out this journal, you probably already know how negative self-talk has made an undesirable impact on your life. You may also know that negative self-talk typically starts with the words, "I can't," "I'll never," "I always (insert a shameful action here)," "I won't," etc. When we hear ourselves say those words enough, the result is that we don't, we won't, and we'll never. Negative self-talk can cause you to worry more and try less. It can tear down your confidence and self-esteem. It often interferes with relationships and gets in the way of success in work. It very well may be the reason you can't seem to meet those life goals you've been agonizing over. You may think this kind of self-talk is just "tough love," almost like a drill sergeant who covertly has your best interests at heart. But negative self-talk tends to deflate rather than motivate, regardless of the intent.

If negative self-talk is the poison, then positive self-talk is the antidote. Positive self-talk can increase self-esteem, improve self-image, and grow self-efficacy. Positive self-talk starts with phrases like "I'm capable of," "I have the power to," "I can," etc. (Think the Richard Simmons of cognitive processes.) Studies show that positive self-talk can have a range of positive outcomes, from sustained weight loss to a decrease in clinical depression and anxiety. People can't experience much joy in their lives if there's an unrelenting naysayer narrating the journey, right? If negative self-talk deflates, positive self-talk rescues and reinvigorates.

Remember, it takes time to develop and become a well-oiled, positive-self-talk machine. If you're struggling with negative thought patterns, recognize that developing those patterns in the first place required practice and implementation; you just may not be cognizant of how you got to that point. And while positive self-talk might not come naturally at first, with practice, it can happen just as effortlessly as the current negative messages you're sending yourself.

So, let's bring it back to why you're here and how this journal can be useful to you. Here, you'll find various exercises and affirmations that work in tandem to change your self-talk for the better. The exercises are progressive. They serve as a step-by-step guide to gaining awareness into your thought processes, giving you tools to bring more positive self-talk into your life. Many of the journal's questions are designed for you to respond directly on the page. There are also affirmations—positive self-statements—throughout the journal for you to adopt and incorporate into your life. Affirmations pick up momentum the more we say them to ourselves. They offer easy ways to increase positive self-talk, and there is a lot of research that shows how effective they are in creating change in our lives through persistent repetition. If the exercises are the wheels on this journey, the affirmations are the gas. And we need both to get where we want to go.

Let's take a moment to unpack the affirmations piece. I know some people consider affirmations unbelievable and feel silly when practicing them. I've worked with lots of clients that really struggle with buying in to these statements, especially when they don't feel connected to the words when they first say them. I have to confess that I, too, felt this way prior to writing this journal. But in the midst of my writing, I began to incorporate the affirmations into my own life by choosing one each week and using it during challenging moments. I meditated on my chosen affirmation and repeated it as many times throughout the day as I could remember—even when that other voice in my brain was being cynical about it. And wouldn't you know, the more I did this, the more I found ways in my life that the affirmations were accurate. The affirmations then began to guide my thought processes and experiences—with myself, others, and the world. All it took was for me to give myself permission to believe in them.

Changing self-talk is at the heart of the work I do, and it's obviously at the heart of this journal. If we don't believe in our ability to accomplish something, we simply won't do it. But if we allow ourselves to be encouraged and challenged, the chance of successfully experiencing change increases exponentially. That being said, I need you to commit to believing in the possibility that changing your self-talk will make a positive impact on you. This commitment is entirely up to you. While we may not have control over our automatic, subconscious thoughts, we do have control over whether to buy in to these thoughts and actively try to change them. It requires dedication to believe in the possibility that using the exercises and affirmations in this journal will ultimately have a lasting impact on your psyche and life overall. If you give yourself the opportunity to practice in earnest, your thought process will change for the better and you'll have to work less to convince yourself of the good things—talking kindly to yourself will become second nature.

You have the power to change your narrative. All you have to do is believe in this power and your own potential. Ready? Let's begin.

What brought you here?

What do you want to accomplish by using this journal? These answers serve as a starting point to identify where you're coming from and why you're truly here. Talk about the role that negative self-talk plays in your life. Think about how this kind of narrative keeps you from being the person you want to be.

What have your internal challenges been because of negative self-talk?

What haven't you been able to accomplish because of it? If your negative self-talk was a person or thing, what would it be and why?

What is getting in the
way of being able to use
positive self-talk more
often in your life?

I AM
CAPABLE.

I AM
COMPETENT.

I AM
CONFIDENT.

Think about a life in which you are only able to talk yourself up (rather than down).

Use this space to narrate how a day in your life might go if positive self-talk was the only player in the game. How would you start your day? How would you handle challenges big and small? What would be the tone and nature of your self-talk? What would your default attitude be? What would you tell yourself in the face of adversity or discomfort?

THERE IS
STOPPING
ACHIEV
GOA

NOTHING
ME FROM
NG MY
LS.

Identify your goals for learning how to talk yourself up.

You can choose just one central goal or come up with many smaller ones. Try to identify at least one SMART goal—within your control—that you can achieve by incorporating positive self-talk into your life. SMART goals are Specific, allow Measurable progress, are Realistic for you to achieve, and can be accomplished in a Timely manner.

Turn the page, read the affirmation aloud, and write it down here in big, bold letters.

Rehearse it frequently throughout the next day or so. When you do, notice—without judgment—how your internal narrative responds.

I BELIEVE IN MY ABILITY

TO
CHANGE
FOR THE
BETTER.

Now think about how you reacted to the affirmation.

Did you embrace it, blow it off, or neither? What did you feel while you repeated the statement, and after? Were your reactions influenced by the world outside of you, or did they seem to come from within, regardless of circumstance? Did you like how you felt after repeating the statement? If not, what was getting in the way of this being a positive experience?

Embracing positive
self-talk starts by identifying
and understanding
your negative self-talk.

Where does this kind of internal talk come from,
and what purpose does it serve? When are you
the most likely to use negative self-talk? What
would you have to lose by giving it up? Perhaps
you're repeating those negative statements out
of fear, shame, guilt, or something else that's
unresolved. Whatever it is, it's important to
recognize that there's a function to this negative
self-talk. Take this time to breathe deeply, examine
the origin of your automatic thoughts, and use
these pages as a safe place to examine the
reasons behind the negative self-talk in your life.

Think of the negative voice in your head as being someone other than yourself.

Name the voice. You could name it after someone you know in real life, or just make up a name. By giving the negative self-talk a name and separating it from yourself, it's easier to hear it as the voice of someone with misguided intentions, instead of buying into the narrative that you are out to sabotage yourself through your own thoughts. Describe the voice's characteristics and qualities. What is its MO? What role is it trying to fulfill? And how might it be convinced to step down from this role?

I HAVE MY OWN BACK

NO
MATTER
WHAT.

Think about someone you know who is gentle and kind. What would they say to support you if you were struggling?

How would they encourage you if you needed a boost? Identify how this person's uplifting voice would impact your life if they were guiding your thoughts on a daily basis. Envision this person giving you positive feedback and using their words to soothe you. Identify how it feels to hear their gentle tones. Now internalize that voice. What name can you give it? How can you embrace it and incorporate it into your inner narrative? The end goal is for this voice to become your own.

I CAN
EXPERIENCE
HAPPINESS

AND
SHARE IT
WITH THOSE
AROUND ME.

It's possible to connect with positive messages received from other people but revert to disbelief when your inner voice says the exact same words.

Isn't that confusing? This is where we get to challenge that dissonance with a little deductive reasoning. If this other person tells you that you're wonderful and you have confidence in their judgment, then you can depend on the validity of the message. So lean into that message from the trusted source, and imagine the message coming to you in your voice rather than theirs.

Think of someone you trust complimenting you.

Get a solid mental image of them saying the compliment. Now, write down the message and strip away the deliverer. Shift your focus away from the emotion it brings up when you hear it, and instead focus on the idea of how aligning with this message would be helpful in your life. Assess the message in terms of its benefit to you. Now, write it down again and, this time, hear your voice expressing it as you read it from the page. Continue this practice of writing and rewriting until you can comfortably say this statement to yourself. If you lose confidence, remind yourself that you can trust the same message from an outside figure.

Using the name of the negative self-talk voice, what evidence do you have that they are right about you?

How do you know the voice is absolutely correct, and is there room for refuting it? Look for evidence to disprove this negative perception. What prevents you from embracing the evidence and accepting it as truth?

I CHOOSE
TO BE
PRESENT

IN ALL
THAT I DO.

Sometimes, the source of our negative self-talk isn't so apparent.

If you are struggling to manage a particular negative feeling but don't know what's driving it, use this space to make some connections. Shift from identifying the feeling (e.g., "I'm feeling overwhelmed") to recognizing the feeling as it relates to yourself ("I'm feeling overwhelmed because I feel incapable in this situation") to identifying the underlying negative self-talk ("I'm not capable"). Finally, change the self-talk so it is more positive while still acknowledging your current feelings ("I know I'm ultimately capable even though I feel overwhelmed right now"). Repeat this exercise with any other emotions you're dealing with, replacing the negative self-statement with a declaration that's based in reality and carries a more positive undertone.

When you are feeling off, hopeless, or low in other ways, it's important to tune in to those feelings—they can act as warning signs that something bigger is happening behind the scenes.

Often, negative self-talk occurs when we feel depleted, anxious, worried, overwhelmed, or insecure. These uncomfortable feelings might be so overwhelming that we can't step outside of them long enough to recognize the interior narrative. But it's often this narrative that drives the emotions, so it helps to pinpoint these feelings and challenge them.

I AM
WORTH MORE
THAN MY
PRODUCTIVITY.

Identify an everyday, versatile, personal affirmation.

You can choose one directly from the journal or construct your own. Whichever you choose, think of it as your trusty go-to for comfort and reassurance. This could be a mantra that grounds you, pumps you up, or both. Next, begin the process of frequently reciting this affirmation— whether it's writing it on the page, repeating it in your head, or saying it aloud. Write about what you notice when you repeat the affirmation over and over. Is there resistance in connecting to the statement, or is there some room for acceptance? Remember, this is a practice, so be gentle with yourself and don't get discouraged if the affirmation doesn't feel natural yet. It might take some time.

I LOVE
CHALLENGES

AND
WHAT I CAN
LEARN FROM
OVERCOMING
THEM.

Take a day and notice how often you engage in negative self-talk.

What do you notice? When does the narration usually come out? What areas in your life are more prone to evoke negative self-talk? Jot down your observations here. Then map out a plan for introducing positive affirmations into the parts of your day when you are most vulnerable to negative internal chatter. There's a beloved mantra that fits here: "If it's predictable, it's preventable." So if you can predict when you might be more prone to negative self-talk, prevent it by arriving equipped with more uplifting self-talk. What plan can you construct to predict and prevent negative self-talk from occurring? When can you strategically insert affirmations or other positive self-talk into your day?

I AM
BEAUTIFUL

JUST THE WAY I AM.

We experience so many thoughts on a daily basis that it's hard to discern which ones to keep and which ones to disregard.

But our thoughts are not necessarily all messages we need to own; we can bypass some while holding on to others that actually serve to enhance our lives. Write down the thoughts you experienced today, and separate them into ones you want to keep and ones you want to let go. This practice empowers you to control what you do with your thoughts and challenges the belief that you have to take ownership of every thought just because it comes from your mind.

Challenging old thoughts with new ones can be confusing at times, as it feels like your thoughts are duking it out.

If you're experiencing difficulty figuring out which thoughts to side with, start by zooming out and looking at both sides. Then identify the more critical voice, and ask whether it has historically been helpful or hurtful to you. If siding with these thoughts has caused you unhappiness, self-doubt, or anxiety, this is not the voice to listen to. Instead, think about instances when you were gentler with yourself. What impact did these thoughts have on your attitude, mood, and subsequent choices? Comparing the two by recalling the impact each typically creates can assist you in siding with one voice versus the other.

I KNOW
WITH TIME
AND
EFFORT,

I CAN
ACHIEVE
ANYTHING.

Pick an affirmation and begin incorporating it into your daily life.

How do you feel about yourself when you say this affirmation repeatedly? How does it change your attitude? Is it easy to incorporate into your daily routine, or do you catch yourself forgetting? How does it feel to buy into the affirmation? Identify which part of yourself is giving you permission to believe the affirmation and which part is reticent to connect with it.

I CHO

REACH

BETTER

SE TO

FOR A

EELING.

Write out all the negative self-statements you made today.

Reflect on how you felt as a result of these statements. Did they motivate or deflate? What is tempting about continuing to hold on to these statements? What is easy to leave behind by detaching from the negativity?

Write out all the positive self-statements you made today.

These can be applications of your affirmations or rebuttals to negative self-statements.

Identify how these positive self-statements made you feel.

What impact did they make? Did they deflate or reinvigorate you? What's challenging about believing these statements? What is easy about believing these statements?

Choose or create an affirmation.

Write it out on the page as many times as possible, but go slowly—pause after each repetition and envision how your life will look when you truly believe this self-statement. Take your time writing each line, leaning into the words and their impact on your life. How would your life change if you intentionally believed the affirmation? What freedom does this statement offer to you? With each repetition, feel yourself embracing the affirmation on a deeper level. What commitment can you make to embodying this affirmation in your life?

I AM
MORE
THAN
ENOUGH.

Create hopeful and kind affirmations while you practice self-forgiveness.

Many people struggle with negative self-talk because it's hard to let go of mistakes. Are you struggling to forgive yourself as a result of perceived failures? Is this contributing to your negative self-talk? Many of us strive for perfection to the point that we forget we're human. The reality is that there's value in our setbacks and we can learn tremendously from our mistakes. Remember that mistakes lead to successes. Identify the mistakes you can't let go of that are holding you back. Then, identify what lessons you learned from those mistakes. Can you take these realizations, give yourself some grace, and create statements that are forgiving and kind? Write out some statements you can connect with.

I AM
WORTHY
OF LOVE.

Identify something negative you've said to yourself, and then write it down, but in opposite form.

For example, if the negative statement is "I'll never be able to get what I want," a positive opposite would be "I deserve good things and get exactly what I need." (Notice how this opposite isn't exact but reverses the original sentiment while still being realistic.) Practice reversing negative statements, visualizing how you can change them into sources of encouragement instead.

Think about an upcoming challenge or stressor in your life.

Describe the situation and—just for comparison's sake—how your past self would have approached it with negative self-talk. How might that situation have turned out for you, and how would you have felt about yourself as a result? Would using negative self-talk encourage or discourage you from approaching this challenge? Now, identify a positive self-statement and guide yourself through the same situation with this improved mentality. Map out how a more supportive internal voice can (and likely will!) alter the situation to your benefit and create a better result.

I O

OBS

BEF

REAC

AN
ERVE
ORE
TING.

Write out objective qualities about yourself that start with the words "You are."

These statements should focus on being kinder, gentler, and more empowering to yourself. Write out as many statements as you can that describe your attributes—characteristics you inherently like about yourself—whether they are strengths, talents, and/or skills. When your negative self-talk pipes up, acknowledge it, but don't let it stop you from continuing your list.

I FEEL POWERFUL AND ALIVE.

When you're feeling low, look back to the "You are" statements you identified on the previous pages as reminders of who you are, rather than how you feel.

Remember, your innate characteristics still belong to you even when you're not at your best, and your feelings are not facts. Identify a situation where you were feeling less than, take a "You are" statement, and use it now to talk yourself up. This is part of the continuous practice of flexing your cognitive self-talk muscles in difficult situations.

I HAVE
ALL THAT
I NEED

TO REACH
MY GOALS.

Let's revisit the goal(s) you set for yourself at the beginning of the journal.

Reflect on your use of affirmations and how it applies to these goals. Have you made any progress? How do you feel about yourself as a result? What's changed so far, and what have been the barriers to change?

MY LIFE IS
UNFOLDING

EXACTLY
HOW IT'S
SUPPOSED
TO.

Change is hard, and you need to have compassion for yourself as you work to make progress.

Even when you know you want to adopt a new process, part of you might not be ready to give up old patterns. Instead of getting frustrated that you're struggling to change your behavior, try to develop some compassion for that part of yourself and what it is afraid to lose. How can you speak to that part of you and calm its fears without giving into negative statements? Set a plan for how you can speak to this part of you in the future and remind it that it's acting on fear instead of facts.

Give yourself an opportunity to take on something with bravery and courage.

Even if trying something new is uncomfortable in the moment, that feeling is only temporary—discomfort in the face of change will certainly pass. Pushing yourself past that reactionary emotion feels so good afterward. Start by identifying something you want to avoid because of the initial scary feeling. Write about why you are avoiding it. What role does your self-talk play in keeping you from tackling this? Next, construct a plan for giving yourself permission to be brave and get through the uncomfortable part of the process. Finally, go forth and conquer your fears!

I CAN
FACE MY
FEARS

WITH
COURAGE
AND
BRAVERY.

Once you've done the scary thing and the event is behind you, use this space to describe how you dealt with what you'd been avoiding.

How did it go when you gave yourself permission to be brave? What was the overall process like, and how did you feel once it was over? Use this space to validate yourself for enduring that "one scary moment" and overcoming it. Way to go, you!

How often do we forget that we have a choice in how things turn out?

Remember that you made a choice to pick up this journal and engage in the process of working toward your goals. You made a choice to change your narrative and the way you talk to yourself, and you can also make a choice about what kind of language to use going forward. As a reminder of your say in the matter, write out a series of statements starting with the words "I choose." They can be virtues, values, mindsets, etc. You can also add the word "today" in front of a statement as a way to begin your day with a positive focus. For example, "Today, I choose peace" or "Today, I choose self-control." Write out as many statements as you can think of and continue to reference them as needed. What will you choose today?

I WILL
USE THE
LESSONS
FROM
YESTERDAY

TO HELP
MYSELF
CONQUER
TODAY.

Create a "relapse prevention plan" for yourself.

Remember that—as with any habit—drifting back to negative self-talk can happen. Identify some warning signs. How will you know when negative self-talk is creeping back in, and what will you do about it? What sort of behaviors or feelings could be indicators of regression? Next, develop a plan for how to bypass this potential backslide. What sources of support can you recruit to help you get back on track? Finally, come up with an emergency affirmation to keep in your tool kit for a rainy day. What should you include in this affirmation to help yourself stay on track?

You made it.
Reflect back on your
whole journey.

Sitting with this information and taking a moment to savor your progress is therapeutic in itself. What did you learn about yourself? In what direction did your journey take you? What was more challenging than you expected, and what was easier than you thought it would be? What did you learn about yourself in the process? What will you continue to take with you as you move forward? What commitment can you make to continue with these practices? How will you thrive on this journey, and what excites you about your future now?

EACH STEP
IS TAKING ME
TO WHERE I
WANT TO BE,